Also by Clive Lewis OBE DL

The Definitive Guide to Workplace Mediation

Win Win: Resolving Workplace Conflict: 12 Stories

Workplace Mediation Skills

Performance Management

Work-Life Balance

Bouncing Back from Redundancy

Looking for Your Next Job?

Leadership with Compassion

Difficult Conversations in Dementia

Index

Introduction   Page 1

Step 1 - Recognise the need   Page 7

Step 2 – Prepare   Page 12

Step 3 – Get advice or support   Page 16

Step 4 – Be courageous   Page 20

Step 5 – E-void   Page 24

Step 6 – Be professional   Page 28

Step 7 – Listen   Page 33

Step 8 – Let it go   Page 37

Step 9 – Keep going   Page 41

Step 10 – Make it a lifestyle   Page 44

Influence and Persuasion   Page 47

Case studies   Page 58

Conclusion   Page 64

References   Page 66

Order form   Page 68

About the author   Page 69

Difficult Conversations

10 Steps to Becoming a Tackler not a Dodger

Clive Lewis

Introduction

In the 21st century, difficult conversations are everywhere. Whether we're at home, at work or in a social situation, unwanted subjects can suddenly be raised which demand us to do either one of two things – to tackle the conversation or to dodge it. All of us react in different ways. Indeed some may choose to tackle one subject and dodge the next, but all too often in the current climate, those in management positions, whose job it is to deal with potentially difficult or damaging situations, are dodging more than they are tackling – 60% of them according to a recent study of 1,000 employees[1].

We all have to face difficult conversations in our lives, both at work and at home, which we either dodge (avoid) or tackle (deal with).

This unwillingness to tackle problematic issues isn't the preserve of managers however – all of us at some point are guilty of not having 'that conversation', be it with a work colleague, a loved one, a manager, a supplier or a customer. On all of these levels, dodging issues rather than tackling them often has a derogatory effect on the morale of individuals and the health of relationships which, in terms of a department or team, leads to reduced productivity and output, which then has an obvious knock-on effect for the organisation as a whole. Not only that, those directly involved in a workplace conflict that continues unchallenged may begin to suffer everything from sleepless nights to

Many managers are dodging when they should be tackling, which impacts negatively on their team and thus the organisation as a whole.

We're all guilty of dodging now and again, but many of us realise the risks of doing it serially.

weight loss to depression, leading to extended periods of absence from work. You can, I'm sure, draw your own parallels to personal relationships. Allied to this, the dodger is more personally affected by his or her actions than the tackler. The tackler deals with a situation appropriately, however unpleasant it may be, and tries to move on, whereas the dodger merely adds another stone to their already heavy bag of people and situations to avoid whilst they try and find a place to hide – a bag that weighs them down every minute of every day and represents a prime recipe for stress and ill-health. When the bag becomes too heavy, even the best dodgers run out of places to hide.

Dodging difficult conversations can lead to workplace conflict.

Dodging, rather than tackling difficult conversations can affect the health of all the individuals involved as well as the business.

The pace and dynamic of the modern workplace has had a twofold effect on the presence of difficult conversations – they are both required and avoided more than ever before. In a world where competition is cutthroat, different generations have different ways of working and employee performance can be monitored and scrutinised to the nth degree. The modern day manager can be seen as part manager, part fire-fighter attempting to extinguish all the various conflagrations that crop up throughout the average working day, addressing everything from colleague disputes to missed targets. Successful companies therefore require managers who are able and willing to deal with these situations as and when they arrive.

Difficult conversations are both required and avoided more than ever before, with high pressure decisions being made every day. Some companies don't adequately train their staff in dealing with these issues.

However, a 2010 survey found that over two thirds (72%) of line managers were uncomfortable having difficult conversations[2]. An incredible statistic that bears up findings that the cost of conflict to UK businesses per year is a staggering £33bn, of which almost £19.5bn (59%) relates to internal conflict, such as problems with line managers and colleagues[1]. With these kinds of figures, it is more than easy to picture the amount of lost productivity in offices up and down the land due to managers dodging rather than tackling.

Dodger managers cost the UK economy billions of pounds a year.

So why *do* we dodge when tackling is clearly the most effective method of dealing with potential conflict? Our emotional reactions to such situations are similar to our physical reactions when presented with danger – fight or flight. Our basis for decision making is obviously different than when confronted by danger, in that difficult conversations are rarely likely to endanger our wellbeing at a physical level, but we know inherently what is 'bad' for us and will act in either of those two instinctive manners. Choosing to 'fight', to have the difficult conversation and get it out of the way, is not something that comes naturally to many people, but those who learn to adopt the mentality, soon discover that it provides the basis for much easier and more productive working and social relationships and therefore greater levels of success than those who skirt around issues. Tackler managers become more

How we deal with difficult conversations is directly related to our individual 'fight or flight' instincts.

Tacklers are generally able to move upwards quicker in an organisation than dodgers.

respected and trusted by colleagues and subordinates who know that if they report a problem something will be done about it, as opposed to dodger managers who leave problems to fester and therefore damage team morale in the long run. For those aiming for promotion to managerial positions, effective tackling is a sure-fire way to get noticed – for the right reasons.

Tacklers become more trusted and respected by colleagues, subordinates and managers, leading to a higher chance of success.

This handbook aims to provide those who regularly find themselves consciously failing to address difficult issues or shying away from potentially awkward conversations with 10 steps to follow in order to tackle these situations head on. They are:

Before:	Recognise the need
	Prepare
	Get advice or support
	Be courageous
	E-void
During:	Be professional
	Listen
After:	Let it go
	Keep going
	Make it a lifestyle

The ten steps in this handbook will help those who continually find themselves avoiding difficult or awkward conversation both professionally and personally.

The steps will be based around professional relationships and situations, but the principles involved will work just as well with personal relationships too.

This handbook won't have your difficult conversation for you, but it will act as a guide, helping you through the various stages of the conversation from planning to execution to post meeting, until you're experienced enough to detect and deal with impending issues both at work and home without needing to refer to it. Think of it as learning a new recipe – initially you'll need to follow the instructions, but soon you'll be adding your own touches and doing it without thinking.

Using this guide will allow you to become a confident tackler in no time.

There is one thing dodgers enjoy that tacklers don't – that joyous feeling of relief when something that has been weighing them down is finally resolved, either by themselves or, more often, by a third party. As a difficult conversation tackler, you will probably have to grow to live without that particular feeling, but the better news is that you won't have to have the weights dropped onto you in the first place. You won't have to pretend you didn't get that email or voicemail, you won't have to find excuses for not being able to sit down and meet with someone, you won't have to alter your course to the photocopier because of who you might bump in to on the way. Instead of drowning under the weight of these constant pressures you'll be free to walk, speak to and meet with anyone you want because you are a tackler, not a dodger. Does that sound appealing? Then let's get started.

Once you've learned how to tackle you won't have to fear any emails, phone calls or unexpected visits ever again.

"Every duty which is bidden to wait returns with seven fresh duties at its back."

Charles Kingsley

"Putting off an easy thing makes it hard. Putting off a hard thing makes it impossible."

George Claude Lorimer

"The dread of doing a task uses up more time and energy than doing the task itself."

Rita Emmett

Step 1 – Recognise the need

Imagine difficult conversations as small, independent fires. A fire dealt with quickly and effectively will cause minimum damage to all concerned, and repairs can usually be made to patch up the affected areas. It will likely soon be forgotten about and the business can continue as normal. A fire left ignored however will grow and grow, burning upwards as it expands, affecting more and more people in the chain of command and requiring a solution of the requisite size to extinguish it. By this point the damage could be huge, possibly irreparable. In both these scenarios it is highly likely that the shout of 'fire' went up at least once. In the latter scenario, crucially, no-one acted.

Putting out a small fire early on is much easier than tackling a huge blaze months later and results in less damage.

One of the advantages of being a dodger is that you'll probably find that you are better attuned to spotting these fires at the early stages than your tackling counterparts. Unfortunately this early warning system has likely been adapted to enable you to remove yourself from the area of potential conflict before it becomes an issue, rather than allowing you to head these situations off before they manifest themselves. This first step focuses on using this antennae as the platform for turning you into a tackler.

Dodgers are usually better attuned to detecting potentially awkward situations but often don't do anything positive with it.

Where the tackler senses danger and deals with it, the dodger avoids it and hopes it will go away or be dealt with by somebody else. This may work one time out of four or five, but on those other occasions it only takes one person in the affected chain (which grows larger with every ignored opportunity to deal with it) to realise that someone (including you) had the opportunity to stop it and didn't. So your respite is only short lived and the end result is usually worse. Spending your days trying to avoid certain people and hoping you don't get found out is not a fun way of living your life.

As a dodger you may get lucky a couple of times, but generally problems don't resolve themselves.

The first hurdle to clear then is this almost automatic reaction to defer, put off, sideline or avoid. When confronted by the need to engage in something unpleasant there are usually two opposing forces at work – your own desire to avoid a potentially unpleasant experience pitted against the desire (or the need, depending on your position) to have the situation resolved and dealt with. Needless to say, dodgers often set their self-preservation above the need to have the situation resolved. Interestingly, the weighing up of these odds usually doesn't even occur to a tackler. They don't perform the same mental balancing act before dealing with the situation, they just act. Although this process isn't 100% effective (certain 'gung-ho' tacklers could in fact learn a thing or two from the dodgers on this front), but what you can guarantee is that concerns about any unpleasantness

Tacklers very rarely consider the potential unpleasantness of a conversation that needs dealing with. In fact they tend to deal with it before any negative thoughts get time to settle.

fall so far down their list of priorities that they usually don't feature. To them there is no decision to make – they want the situation addressed, dealt with and in the past. Now of course to a dodger this is easier said than done, but this is the kind of mentality you may, in time, find yourself adopting.

Negative thoughts about a difficult meeting or conversation are usually the first step on the dodger's ladder to avoidance. Misery loves company, so they say, and this is true with dodging – one negative thought is usually followed by another and another and another until you've dug yourself into a pit of irrational negative emotion associated with the event so deep, that you'll find it impossible to get out of. Suddenly the thought of tackling makes you physically ill. Tacklers are adept at setting these fears aside the moment they surface, to the point where, with practice, thoughts of their own discomfort come a distant second, or third, to their sense of duty and responsibility. A good way to begin thinking like a tackler is to try and rationalise these thoughts. With every negative connotation, consider seeing things objectively and analyse:

a) how likely that problem is to arise
b) how you might effectively counter it
c) how bad it *really* is in the great scheme of things

Just one or two negative thoughts and fears, rational or otherwise, will quickly multiply and leave you with no desire to tackle the situation at all.

With practice you'll soon be able to block out your fears or, at best, rationalise them one by one.

By playing the ghost buster you will help burst these bubbles of fear that you associate with such events, exploding the myths you have believed yourself for so long. There is a high probability that the things you fear are in fact largely insignificant when looked at objectively, especially if you plan for their arrival in advance. Soon you'll be wondering what it was you were worried about, and you'll be ready to tackle the situation.

Many fears about difficult conversations prove to be unfounded and are all in the imagination.

The next nine stages will guide you through conducting difficult conversations, but this first stage is entirely down to you. Seeing dodging as an unpleasant habit that you want to kick is a good way to look at it. It is a frame of mind that's holding you back, that's stopping you from taking charge of situations and moving on with your life and career. Perhaps events are controlling you where you need to be controlling them. Needless to say, dodgers are very rarely, if ever, as successful as tacklers – how can they be? If you want to stop running, if you want to make a stand and prove to yourself that you can do it, then recognising and accepting the need to have a difficult conversation represents the most important of steps.

Like kicking a habit, this process requires willpower. You can only be a tackler if you really want to.

"In preparing for battle I have always found that plans are useless, but planning is indispensable."

Dwight D Eisenhower

"Being unprepared heightens nerves."

James Galway

"The wise man bridges the gap by laying out the path by means of which he can get from where he is to where he wants to go."

John Pierpont Morgan

Step 2 - Prepare

As many of us know from often bitter experience, jumping into a difficult conversation unprepared usually ends in one of a number of unpleasant ways. Having these sorts of conversations thrust upon us catches us off guard, makes us panic and forces us to try and make sense of all the thoughts that come bounding into our head in that moment, which regularly results in a jumble of mixed messages and nothing being cleared up.

Lack of adequate preparation will usually yield a much less productive and more troubling conversation.

Planning won't answer all your prayers, but it will make the impending conversation far easier for you to engage in.

An easy way to prepare for a difficult conversation is to liken it to a time you split from a partner, be it in a romantic or a professional sense. There comes a point where we all begin to wonder how we will react if we bump into them on the street. What should we say? How should we sound? How do we want to come across? What do we want our lasting impression to be etc? These same principles can help you when it comes to difficult conversations in other spheres and will help drive your actions during the discussion. As with these post break-up meetings you need to have a clear idea of what you want out of the discussion before you enter it. Do you need to come out knowing certain information? Are you seeking a change in the other party's behaviour? Will you be expected to negotiate towards an agreement? Even if you're open minded

Plan a difficult conversation like you would a potential meeting with a recent ex – What points do you want to make? How do you want to come across etc?

Always have in mind what you want your end goal to be – it will drive your subconscious thoughts and actions.

and don't know what outcome you want, you need to be prepared so you can work towards that eventuality. Keeping in mind what you want to achieve will subconsciously drive your body language and tone of voice, whilst your conscious thoughts look after the actual words you're saying.

One important thing to remember with the preparation aspect is that you get your facts right. Reeling off unsubstantiated gossip when trying to have a serious discussion is going to undermine your position, so ensure that you stick to what you know, or at least strongly suspect, to be true. Facts, particularly those backed up with evidence, can form the backbone of your argument and can often speak for themselves, but the tricky part can come if you're investigating unsubstantiated claims or complaints. In these cases it might be wise to prepare a shortened, diluted version of what has been passed to you and ask the individual for an explanation of these events. Their response, and the way in which they deliver it, should give you an indication of how close to the truth you are. We will touch more on this area in step 7.

Referring to facts and information will take the pressure off you – but make sure you know they are correct!

Many fears regarding difficult conversations stem from concern about the reactions of the individual(s) being addressed; fears of anger, bitterness, high emotion, rejection and other potentially uncomfortable

Preparing for the likely reaction(s) will help you deal with them if and when they come.

responses that one would rather not risk. There is no denying that, in some situations, these fears will be realised, but preparing for the likely reaction in advance and planning what to do or say if they occur can ease the burden tremendously. Facts again can be useful here. Providing individuals with any pertinent data or information that has necessitated the meeting takes the blame off you personally and shifts it onto the 'evidence' itself.

Peer-peer scenarios are always more unpleasant than manager-employee ones because of the equal status of all those involved, so preparation here is even more important. Practicing what you need to say, perhaps with an impartial third party, can be a very useful way of measuring how you're coming across and can help you find the right wording so you sound like the concerned team member that you (hopefully) are. Trying to think of the discussion as a meaningful conversation with purpose, rather than a difficult conversation may help. Remember, your version of subtle may not be someone else's. Someone who has read and rehearsed their lines will be much better equipped, much more relaxed and much more focused on the intended outcome than someone who is trying to attempt a difficult conversation ad-hoc. Getting into the habit of regular, effective preparation will turn you into a tackler in no time.

Peer-peer scenarios have to be handled differently to manager-employee. Avoid trying to appear more senior than them – use team words ('us', 'we') rather than personal ('me, 'I').

Practice your lines. Run through what you intend to say with an appropriate third party. Remember, your version of tact may not be everyone's!

"To accept good advice is but to increase one's own ability."

Johann Wolfgang von Goethe

"Many receive advice, only the wise profit from it."

Publilius Syrus

"Advice is seldom welcome, and those who need it the most, like it the least."

Lord Chesterfield

Step 3 – Get advice or support

Getting help isn't as daunting a task as you might think – you've done it yourself in fact, by buying this book. Yet somehow asking someone for help face to face isn't quite as easy as that. The chances are that, whatever the situation you're trying to address, someone else has been through it – probably within your own organisation. There are very few incidents that occur in the workplace that are completely original. This means that out there somewhere is someone who has been through what you are going through and has come out the other side. So why not ask for their help, or at least learn from their mistakes?

Someone you know, either at work or socially, has probably gone through what you're about to. Learn from others' mistakes.

Some feel that they are too proud to ask for advice, an action which usually leads to a larger fall if the discussion doesn't end amicably, or at least productively. The fate of the meeting is in your hands, and a badly handled one, where advice was readily available will have far worse repercussions than the opposite. It isn't damaging to one's pride to ask for advice or help, but it is damaging to have people talking about how badly you handled a specific situation. A good tackler seeks information from as many sources as possible before making their move, as opposed to the person who barges in and tactlessly announces their thoughts.

Asking for help is not a sign of weakness. It is a sign that you're putting success first.

A badly handled meeting where advice was available but not taken will reflect very poorly.

Help needn't even come from someone related to the issue. A friend, partner or family member may have been in your position, or even the position of those you need to have the difficult conversation with. Knowing what to avoid or look out for beforehand will aid your cause considerably. If you have pinpointed someone who may be able to help, but you can't bring yourself to ask directly, get into conversation about something else and casually slip in that you have the upcoming matter to deal with. If you have a good relationship with the person they will likely be only too glad to relay their experiences, and if you don't have a good relationship with them then you probably wouldn't be talking to them in the first place!

If you feel uncomfortable asking directly, casually slip your upcoming discussion into conversation with someone you think may be able to help.

The internet too is a great source of advice and information. Some of it isn't to be trusted of course, but there are dozens of management forums out there with ideas and suggestions of how to deal with a whole range of issues. Again, there is no harm in researching what other people have done in your situation – anonymously as far as websites and forums go. You may even see some suggestions that you can instantly tell are good or bad, which shows you have the right instincts. Don't rely wholly on mediums such as the internet, but they are a useful starting point.

Use resources such as books, magazines, websites and forums – but don't rely on them.

Regardless of how you go about it, getting advice can help enormously with the preparation of your forthcoming conversation. Knowing what to definitely avoid or include beforehand can assist greatly in circumventing a number of issues. It is important to think how you will be able to make the other person feel safe so that they don't feel obliged to respond combatively. We all have different levels of personal pride, but you will probably find that avoiding seeking help and just ploughing on regardless will ensure you go down in the estimations of all those concerned if the meeting doesn't go well.

Getting advice can aid your planning process greatly, outlining potential pitfalls you may not otherwise have seen.

"You can conquer almost any fear if you will only make up your mind to do so. For remember, fear doesn't exist anywhere except in the mind."

Dale Carnegie

"An invincible determination can accomplish almost anything and in this lies the great distinction between great men and little men."

Thomas Fuller

"Confront your fears, list them, get to know them, and only then will you be able to put them aside and move ahead."

Jerry Gillies

Step 4 – Be courageous

We all experience cold feet from time to time, from a holiday bungee jump to approaching someone in a bar. Even tacklers who pride themselves on their ability to avoid procrastination get stuck every now and again. Decisions based purely on private inclination are far easier to back out of than those that someone is urging you undertake. Sometimes you can do all the planning and preparation you like but when it comes to the moment, as many jilted brides and grooms can attest, it all gets too much and you fear that you can't go through with it.

We all suffer from cold feet now and again, no matter how much preparation work we have done.

Dodgers are adept at searching for ways out of situations – even the smallest seed of doubt will be used as an excuse not to go through with something potentially unpleasant. But what can be done to combat these moments of doubt? The first thing to remember is to trust yourself and your planning. If you've followed the steps in this handbook, or a similar process, then you should have everything ready for your conversation – what you want to get across, how you want to do it and the reactions you're likely to face. With all these in mind the chances of anything unexpected happening are greatly reduced, so fear of anything related to these matters should be equally lowered. If you still find yourself incapable of taking

Dodgers typically find themselves searching for ways out of pressure situations. Don't give in!

Trust in your planning. If you've done enough then less will surprise you.

the necessary steps towards achieving your goal, try to isolate and identify the individual concerns before they manifest themselves and overrule any determination you have conjured up in order to get to this point. Once you have identified the areas concerning you, think back to your preparation for the meeting and how you planned to deal with those particular issues. This should then reassure you that you have planned adequately for the meeting, thus enabling you to trust the plans you have put in place.

On some occasions it's not as easy as isolating one particular emotion – there's just that feeling in the pit of your stomach that won't let your legs move in the direction of the person you need to meet with. There is a very good reason for this. As animals we're programmed to avoid danger at all costs, and so putting yourself in a situation where you feel at risk is something your body isn't going to let you do easily. This is where willpower and determination come into play – a case of mind over matter. You're going to have to force your body onwards. To help achieve this, visualise that moment where you walk out of the office or meeting room with the matter resolved. Imagine the relief you will feel when that issue is dealt with and out of the way. That feeling may be only minutes or even seconds away, and with all the preparation you've done you have next to nothing to worry about.

Try isolating, identifying and rationalising your individual concerns. In the light of analysis, they will seem much less scary.

A stubborn body can be overruled by a more determined mind. Visualise the moment that the discussion will be concluded. You could be only minutes away from that.

To combat more stubborn resistance, it may help to focus on what has prompted you to have this meeting in the first place. If you don't resolve it, what will the consequences be? Chances are they will be more unpleasant than just dealing with it now. After all, if you back out you'll have to go through all this again but with added pressure.

If first time round is uncomfortable, second, third and fourth times round will be hell! Lessen your pain and get it done!

All these factors can sometimes add up to an acceptance that really you have no choice but to go through with it. Great! You're becoming a tackler!

"A single conversation across the table with a wise person is worth a month's study of books."

Chinese Proverb

"I've always believed that a lot of the trouble in the world would disappear if we were talking to each other instead of about each other."

Ronald Reagan

"The workforce reduction notification is currently in progress. Unfortunately your position is one that has been eliminated."

Email to RadioShack employees, 2006

Step 5 – E-void

Electronic communications have revolutionised the way we work. International colleagues are now just an email away, whilst even meetings can be virtual rather than real life. Human beings are naturally social animals however, and such quick, radical changes to the way we interact is not something that we have adequately adapted to yet – the written word, if not communicated by someone up to the task, can be badly misconstrued; badly phrased emails, memos or text messages have been the catalyst for many a workplace discordance.

Email is great, but not suitable for conducting difficult conversations. Dealing with a difficult conversation in this manner is disrespectful and unprofessional.

Written communication also fails to take into consideration the tone of voice, personality and body language of the person with whom we are interacting, essential tools for working out the other party's state of mind and, crucially, adapting our style to fit. With an email the recipient is just a blank canvas, devoid of emotion, whereas the same person in a face to face meeting might reveal a more sensitive side, requiring flexible handling rather than a monotone email that can be misinterpreted. Dealing with a difficult or sensitive matter by email would be seen as disrespectful by many and would be frowned upon by most companies, so the only way to really deal with difficult conversations is face to face, or over the

In an email the other party can seem like a blank, emotionless canvas, whereas this is often not the case.

Some issues can be dealt with over the phone, but face to face meeting should be your priority.

phone if this genuinely isn't a possibility. If you're in any doubt about this, put yourself in the other party's shoes and consider how you would feel if you were communicated to by email on the subject in hand.

Put yourself in the other party's shoes – how would you feel if you were emailed about the issue you need to discuss?

As we have discussed in a previous section, the prolific use of email has enabled those who tend to avoid confrontations to hide behind server errors, junk mail filters or good old-fashioned unspecified "email problems". If you're a dodger you'll be well used to these techniques whereas a tackler would act upon such an email and clear up the issue as soon as possible. Sometimes a quick reply is all it takes to resolve a matter, but tacklers would think nothing of picking up the phone and speaking to that person straight away if that was what the situation required – something a dodger would rarely countenance when an email would do, even if it just prolonged the matter. Dodgers tend to almost always prefer electronic interaction to human interaction, even if it takes longer to sort their issue out. A good test is to ask yourself if, when say cancelling a mobile phone contract, you would prefer to take an hour to do it online or five minutes over the phone, knowing that the result will be the same. Sacrificing time at the expense of avoiding a potentially awkward conversation is a hallmark of a dodger. If this is you, think how much time you would have saved in the last month alone if

The time it takes to hide behind technical glitches and non-receipt of emails could be used to actually sort out the problem once and for all.

Dodgers usually prefer impersonal methods of problem solving even if it takes much longer.

you'd have dealt with things in the most efficient way, rather than the way of least inconvenience to you.

A quick phone call or face to face visit to thrash things out can save time, energy and resources in the short term as well as the long term. Trying to sweep something under the carpet raises the prospect of further difficult conversations every time someone tries to revive the issue, and with every passing opportunity to set up that meeting or make that phone call the bubble grows and grows. In many of the conflicts I've mediated, the majority of the problems could have been avoided if one of the parties had had the wherewithal to deal with the issue in the correct manner from the outset rather than try to hide it. This would have saved the organisation thousands of pounds in fees, sick pay and lost working hours. So the next time an email drops into your inbox, try to deal with it in the manner that will result in the fastest, most appropriate resolution, not the way that feels most comfortable to you.

A quick phone call or personal visit can replace hours of electronic toing, froing and worrying.

Dealing with an issue quickly but unprofessionally is just as bad as not doing anything. Think carefully about the gravity of the forthcoming discussion before you decide on a method of communication.

"Professionalism: It's not the job you do, it's how you do the job."

Anonymous

"Tact is the art of making a point without making an enemy."

Sir Isaac Newton

"Do unto others as you would have others do unto you."

Matthew 7:12

Step 6 – Be professional

For those who shy away from difficult conversations, knowing what to say and what to avoid can be the most difficult part to master. You worry about phraseology, how you'll come across and the reactions you'll garner amongst other things. Whilst you can only predict the other party's responses to a point, there are a number of things you can do to drive the direction of the conversation and limit the fallout.

Finding the right words to say is a major headache for both tacklers and dodgers when it comes to difficult conversations.

The idiom that 'it's not what you say but how you say it that matters' is never truer here, and it is an excellent tag line to keep at the forefront of your exchanges. As a starting point, put yourself in the position of the person you are due to talk to. How would *you* like to be addressed about the matter? What specific words or terms would *you* not want to hear? What would make *you* either clam up or spill the beans? Keep these in mind for your meeting and *you* shouldn't go far wrong. Your conversation could of course be based on anything – you could be a manager discussing poor performance with an employee or a colleague consoling another colleague on recent bad news – but the basics are more or less the same.

Keep in mind that it's not what you say but how you say it that matters.

Put yourself in the other party's shoes. What would you not want to have somebody say to you?

- **Hold the meeting in private** – it sounds obvious, but some managers have been known to conduct conversations of a delicate

Holding the meeting in private shows professionalism.

nature in corridors or even at desks in front of other colleagues. A private place, preferably a meeting room or at least a secluded part of the building where you will not be interrupted, will give the other party the confidence that they won't be overheard. They will also appreciate your candour and will see you as the professional you are.

- **Maintain eye contact** – there is nothing more frustrating than talking to someone who won't keep eye contact with you. Eye contact creates a bond and encourages trust and sincerity between you, as well as allowing you to judge the other party's reactions and thus better plan your own response.

Maintaining eye contact fosters trust and sincerity.

- **Be tactful** – avoid referring to the object of your discussion with strong, direct or explicit language. If needs be, research alternatives to use beforehand and stick to them. Example: "It has been mentioned that your appearance isn't quite what we expect at this organisation" **not** "You look messy – do something about it".

Avoiding strong, direct or explicit language is almost always essential.

- **Avoid accusations** – where possible, avoid direct accusations without first hand evidence. A third party may not have seen

Making unproven allegations will ensure a frosty, unproductive meeting.

what they think they saw, so gently ask for an explanation. Example: "We've heard reports of smoking in the toilets. Do you know anything about this?" **not** "you were seen smoking in the toilets."

Make sure the other party understands what is expected of them.

- **Don't make a big deal of it** – except for conversations involving some form of discipline, make as little of the issue as you can. Mention specific incidents on as few occasions as possible – just state your case and move on to a resolution. If disciplining is required, make sure that the other party understands fully what their expected conduct is before they leave, but again try not to ram the point home.

Avoid bringing anyone else into the discussion. It doesn't matter who it came from originally, it's coming from you now.

- **Don't mention other people** – if you are following up complaints from other people, do not refer to them, either by name or department. This only leads to acrimony and possible retribution. Example: "It has been brought to my attention that…" **not** "employee A saw you…"

Remaining on their side and offering help, especially in a manager-employee relationship, is vital. Don't just criticise.

- **Offer help, don't just criticise** – of course someone needs to know if they're doing something wrong, but leaving the meeting on a negative tone won't help anybody. Offer them help, or prepare some potential solutions in advance – if appropriate.

- **Keep on track** – as part of the preparation you should already have an idea in mind of how you want the meeting to progress and what you want the resolution to be. Keep this in mind and try and gently steer the conversation in this direction.

Keeping to the targets you outlined before the meeting – know how you want it to end and stay on that path.

- **Leave on a positive** – as previously mentioned, leaving a difficult conversation on a negative note rarely benefits anyone. End the conversation by looking toward the future, saying that you have faith that the other party can carry through any measures you have discussed. Agree to put the matter behind you. Example: At the end of the meeting you could say something like "now we have talked about the situation, let's get on with the business of the day" **not** "don't forget what I said – I'll be watching".

Always leave the meeting on a positive note, looking to the future not the past.

If all else fails, put yourself in their place!

Adequate preparation combined with these guidelines should see your meeting go relatively smoothly, no matter what the subject matter. Any topic can be tackled if the groundwork is done and professionalism is retained at all times. And again, if you're in any doubt, put yourself in the other person's place.

"There is no such thing as a worthless conversation, provided you know what to listen for. And questions are the breath of life for a conversation."

James Nathan Miller

"Seek first to understand, then to be understood."

Dr Stephen Covey

"Courage is what it takes to stand up and speak; courage is also what it takes to sit down and listen."

Winston Churchill

Step 7 - Listen

Many people underestimate the importance of listening. I regularly stress the fact that a large percentage of the mediations I deal with on a daily basis could have been avoided if all the parties involved had been listened to from the outset. A quick conversation to nip arising issues in the bud can save time, effort, money and, most importantly, protect the health of those concerned. Unfortunately many of us favour getting our point across rather than listening to the thoughts of others and fail to fully understand what someone may be saying, or trying to say to us. This has obvious repercussions for conversations of the type we are discussing.

The importance of listening is often underestimated, and few managers get adequate training.

Many of us talk when we should be listening, especially in a fast-paced, information filled world.

By this time, with all the necessary planning under your belt, it can sometimes feel very tempting to launch into your meeting, ticking off your list of points one by one until you've addressed them all and then leave, thinking you've had your difficult conversation. This however would be nothing but a nervous lecture. You should always be prepared to allow time for the other person to have their say. Actually listening to someone, as opposed to just hearing them, is essential on two levels. Firstly, from a managerial perspective, it encourages employees to feel valued – a crucial ingredient in organisational success. A constantly busy,

With all your planning done, it can be tempting to just get into your meeting and let fly. This should be avoided!

Being listened to makes us feel valued, both as people and employees.

brusque or inattentive manager will quickly be assumed to be uninterested in team issues, untrustworthy and may be sidestepped in the future. For managers, taking the time to listen to team or individual issues, even if you can't deal with them right away, is a simple yet powerful way of encouraging trust amongst staff – as long as it is followed up with action at some point. A manager who avoids opportunities to listen, listens inattentively or promises action but doesn't deliver will quickly become the subject of unfavourable reports from team members.

Secondly, as we have seen, anticipated reactions from the other party should be prepared for, but things don't always pan out as we expect. A really successful tackler will go into a meeting with an open mind, waiting to hear what the other party has to say before reacting themselves. It is therefore important that you really take on board what the other person has to say and alter your response accordingly, rather than just reeling off the pre-planned response you think matches it closest. Listening in this fashion doesn't just involve hearing the words coming out of their mouth, it involves studying their body language, their facial expressions and trying to read between the lines if they are being particularly cagey. Actively listening to and watching them will tell you much more than you think, which you can then use to pursue certain areas

Inattentive and unsympathetic managers will quickly lose the support of their team.

When cornered, many dodgers will promise action in order to get themselves out of the situation but often fail to deliver. Only promise action if you intend to deliver it.

Top tacklers go into meetings with open minds and deal with the responses ad-hoc.

When listening, look for body language, tone of voice and other sub-conscious signals. What is being said may not reflect the entire truth.

and avoid others in order to reach the resolution you desire. Remember that you may be discussing something so sensitive as time off after a recent bereavement, so there may be times when pursuing certain avenues isn't appropriate. Remember, you are their boss, colleague or customer – not their counsellor. Nevertheless, have your say and then let them have theirs before coming to your conclusions. Encouragement may be required, but be careful not to force them into revealing something they don't want to reveal. After all, it is vital to ensure that they know you are on their side come the end of the meeting.

Always let the other party respond to what you have to say.

Throughout the meeting, ensure that your presence is one ultimately of help and assistance, not punishment. Remain 'on their side'.

"For your own health and well-being, forgiveness is simply the most energy-efficient option. It frees you from the incredibly toxic, debilitating drain of holding a grudge."

Doc Childre & Howard Martin

"Resentment or grudges do no harm to the person against whom you hold these feelings but every day and every night of your life, they are eating at you."

Norman Vincent Peale

"Anger ventilated often hurries toward forgiveness; and concealed often hardens into revenge."

Edward G. Bulwer-Lytton

Step 8 – Let it go

Experiences and conversations stay with us, and sometimes it is the least expected ones that linger the strongest. Some people are born with the capacity to just let things slide and move on with life, whilst others hold on to arguments a little longer than is healthy. Holding a grudge however, especially in a work capacity, can be a powder keg waiting to explode – it can take the slightest spark to set something off that could cause any amount of damage. Letting go of a disagreement, especially if you believe yourself to have been treated unjustly, is an extremely difficult thing to do, but it is the only practical way of resolving conflicts involving people you see on a regular basis.

Holding a grudge is a powder-keg waiting to explode. Inter-personal tensions are divisive but many can be effectively managed if not removed altogether.

A good technique to employ to limit the amount of discord that a difficult conversation can produce is to agree with your meeting attendees that every concern the meeting throws up is to be discussed there and then, that nothing is left unsaid and few tensions, if any, are carried back to the workplace. This allows everyone to clearly visualise the point at which a line will be drawn under the affair and be left in no doubt that it will not be discussed outside of the meeting.

Try and get all the issues dealt with in one go. You don't want negativity spreading back to the office floor.

Despite this being good practice, it is not always met with 100% success. If a meeting doesn't go your way or certain issues are left unresolved in your eyes then it is understandable that you will leave the room with these underlying concerns. In these situations it is of course healthy to have some kind of discourse as keeping everything bottled up inside will inevitably allow a grudge to develop, but ideally this should be limited to a third party or at least someone disconnected with events. Once you have the issue off your chest, you should try your utmost to treat it as history and make a fresh start. You should now treat the other person as you intended them to be changed (if at all) after your discussion. This act of faith shows that you have trust in their ability to move on, thus leading to more chance of it being reciprocated.

Limit post-meeting discussions to third parties. It is healthy to talk about it, but try to put it past you once you've done this.

If you find yourself, either willingly or unwillingly, unable to let go of something that was said or something that happened during a difficult conversation, try to identify the source of your consternation and set up a second discussion about that area – finding out why the other person said it, whether they really meant it and how you can work together to resolve it. If this cannot be acted upon during the meeting itself it should be addressed as soon as possible afterwards before the other party has put the matter behind them.

If something is still bothering you after the discussion, seek another meeting ASAP. The longer you leave it the worse it gets.

A grudge that you can't pinpoint may not actually be the fault of the other person at all; they may have touched on an issue that you yourself have, but because they are the one who raised it you feel like they are accusing you. Being open and honest with yourself, or with a trusted third party, and opening up to the possibility that the problem may in fact be with you may prove fruitful in many ways. The emotions connected to this particular issue are easy enough to detect, but the reasons for those emotions are what need establishing and working on to resolve.

A grudge may be misdirected if you can't work out exactly what's causing it. It could be your hang-ups or issues that someone raised.

"Nothing wilts faster than laurels that have been rested upon."

Percy Bysshe Shelley

"This is just the first step on a long way. We cannot lean back and be complacent."

Wolfgang Bernhard

"Complacency is the biggest challenge. When you've seen success, you can start loosening the belt a little bit..."

Tom Pientok

Step 9 – Keep going

It's great to enjoy your first success as a tackler. It brings a greater sense of freedom and empowerment than you can imagine. Suddenly you feel as if you are controlling events, not having them control you. It really does need just one or two of these victories to make you abolish your dodging ways for good.

Firstly, enjoy your first tackling success!

However, it is unwise to think that just because you have successfully negotiated this first test the issue is over and done with. The resolution you came to, in whichever form it took, will probably require some form of check-up in the not too distant future in order to confirm that the agreed changes, if any were agreed, are being adhered to. It is essential to treat these catch-up meetings (in whatever form they take) with the same passion and attitude as the original conversation. Failing to maintain or enforce any agreements reached, will ultimately render all of your original work pointless.

Many meetings will require follow-ups to ensure progress is being made. These are equally as important and must be approached in the same way as the original meeting.

The proposal of follow-up meetings should be outlined, or even better, firmly agreed during the original meeting. This of course will depend on the context of the original conversation itself. For example, a discussion regarding an employee's appearance is easy to check up on as time progresses, whereas efforts to improve team dynamics will probably require

Outline your plans for follow-up meetings in the original meeting so everybody knows what to expect.

team/individual interviews at some stage down the line. Just how far down the line that is, of course, is entirely up to you, but don't allow your dodging tendency to rear its head and encourage you to put something off for months if it really requires days or weeks. The aim of the game is to deal with things when they need dealing with, so bear this in mind with your decision making on this front.

Don't let the dodger in you rear its head – tackle these meetings head on too.

If your conversation is colleague-colleague rather than manager-employee then suggesting follow-up meetings won't normally be appropriate. It may therefore be a good idea to come to a resolution in the meeting and keep an eye on developments, rather than trying to implement anything 'official'. If things don't improve then it may be worth speaking to someone more senior about the issue.

Follow-up meetings may not be appropriate for colleague-colleague issues. Keep an eye on developments yourself instead.

Whichever side you're approaching the issue from, dealing with it initially may have the desired effect, but be prepared for further conversations along the same lines, if only to check on progress. You can always use the same methods included in this book to facilitate these follow-up meetings.

Use the methods outlined in this book for follow-up meetings if required.

"Observe, record, tabulate, communicate. Use your five senses. Learn to see, learn to hear, learn to feel, learn to smell, and know that by practice alone you can become expert."

William Osler

"Never put off until tomorrow what you can do today."

Thomas Jefferson

"The whole idea of motivation is a trap. Forget motivation. Just do it. Exercise, lose weight, test your blood sugar, or whatever. Do it without motivation. And then, guess what? After you start doing the thing, that's when the motivation comes and makes it easy for you to keep on doing it."

John C Maxwell

Step 10 – Make it a lifestyle

As we saw in the introduction, the feelings of burden and angst that accompany being a dodger and putting things off don't affect tacklers, who instead feel much more welcome feelings of accomplishment and success – a feeling you hopefully either already have or will shortly have. Once you have successfully tackled a difficult scenario and seen the effects, you have laid down a marker for yourself – a platform from which to apply the tackling philosophy to other areas of your life. From this moment, every chance to be a tackler should be taken, to the point where it becomes second nature and you wonder why you procrastinated so much in the first place. You should find in time that the amount of preparation you require becomes less and less as experience combines with instinct to produce speedy resolutions.

Try to reinforce your first tackling success with another one or two, even if they're just everyday things.

You may find in time that you rely less on planning and more on instinct.

For long term success in the dodger-to-tackler transformation, you need to treat your first success not as a one off but the first step on the road. You should of course congratulate yourself, but, as we saw in the previous step, resting on your laurels can be dangerous and render your efforts meaningless. To use the kicking a habit metaphor from earlier, imagine you want to quit smoking (some of you may not have to imagine too hard!). Now visualise every tackle-or-dodge

See dodging as a habit you want to kick – decline each invitation to dodge, no matter how tempting.

confrontation as someone offering you a cigarette. You have two options — to fight the urge and decline the cigarette (tackle the problem) or give in to the urge and accept the cigarette (avoid the problem). Anyone who has tried to give something up - be it smoking or something else, knows how difficult it is to take those first few steps, but they know equally that they are also the most important. Replacing the nagging doubts with practical planning and focusing on the outcome and how good it will feel compared to the guilt and oppression that will come with merely delaying things will hopefully steer you in the right direction when the doubts creep in. The technique of fear rationalisation also works well at this early stage, especially if you have conquered it previously.

When in doubt, identify and rationalise your fears and visualise success.

Once you've tackled a couple of problems you may find that you'll start applying the tackler's mentality to other areas of your life, which is a natural progression. The weekly shop, those little DIY tasks around the house, that paperwork that needs filing — you may well soon find yourself not necessarily *wanting* to do them but at least realising that tackling them is the best way forward. The chances are that before long you'll start putting doubts and negative emotions aside and just get on with it.

You may find that this tackling outlook creeps into everyday life, with the same benefits.

In the workplace, you may also find that those on both sides of the tackling/dodging divide begin to respect you more; dodgers will respect you for doing what they can't, while tacklers will respect you because you have the mentality needed for success. Essentially, you can't lose. Dodgers on the other hand will find the opposite – they are less trusted and respected by both camps. It doesn't take an atomic scientist to work out the long term ramifications of following one of these paths for an extended period of time.

At work, dodgers will respect you for doing what they can't, while fellow tacklers will admire the way you deal with problems.

As we have also seen, dodging problems rather than tackling them adds stress and emotional baggage to our lives – tacklers have much less on their conscience and are generally happier in work as a result. They don't need to avoid anyone or anything, they have fewer worries and concerns and they know that if something awkward pops up they have the confidence and knowledge to assess the situation, deal with it and finish it, all without more delay than necessary, building relationships on the way. And hopefully you've also taken your first step on the path to freedom!

Tackling issues as soon as possible limits the amount of stress you place on yourself, leading to a happier work life.

Say goodbye to hiding from people, phone calls and emails!

A note on Influence and Persuasion

Since the first edition of this book was published in 2011, the accompanying training course has been delivered to thousands of line managers at some of the world's largest and most prestigious organisations. One topic that has been repeatedly asked about is that of influence and persuasion.

> *One topic that has been repeatedly asked about is that of influence and persuasion.*

Influence and persuasion is becoming an increasingly critical competency in today's world of work. The skill is needed, for example, when you work as part of a matrix structure, want to influence peers, lead a team of people or an organisation, or indeed seek to persuade those who are more senior than you. The purpose of adding this chapter in the second edition of the book is to provide some tips and guidance on aspects you might consider to master this area.

> *Influence and persuasion is becoming increasingly critical in today's world of work.*

I recall mediating a dispute between a line manager and her direct report recently. At the end of the session we were talking about some practical things the direct report could do to be able to influence his manager more effectively. Some very basic ideas were tabled such as presenting better quality work and asking a colleague to take a look at a document first before sending on to his manager. Another suggestion included being prepared to sleep on an idea to ensure that it is well thought through prior to presentation and discussion. In another case, a CEO stated how his HR director lost the ability to influence him as he kept on interrupting him and taking his time to talk about the smallest of matters. In a third example, a Board member learnt the hard way about attempting to influence board colleagues. After a first failed attempt for buy-in of a new concept, the HR director suggested that she spend some one-to-one time with executives and non-executives talking through the rationale for her idea prior to the next meeting. She took his advice. To her astonishment, the board meeting simply became a moment for rubber-stamping as she had managed to convince her colleagues of the idea beforehand.

To her astonishment, the board meeting simply became a moment for rubber-stamping as she had managed to convince her colleagues of the idea beforehand.

When you want to increase your ability to influence and persuade, particularly at senior levels, these things matter.

When you want to increase your ability to influence and persuade, particularly at senior levels, these things matter.

There are numerous techniques you can adopt in order to exercise influence and persuasion over others, but I am going to focus on four crucial ones. It goes without saying that some of these factors will be alien to most readers, especially those who are striving to shift away from the dodging mentality, but focusing on the key ones first will hopefully give you the confidence to add more subtle touches when you have the confidence to

There are numerous techniques you can adopt in order to exercise influence and persuasion over others.

do so. After reading this chapter, if you know someone who always seems to get their way, study them where possible and see how many techniques they are using and more importantly, how they utilise them. The best persuaders do this effortlessly, often getting people round to their way of thinking before they realise it!

Trust

There is one thing that is common to every individual, relationship, team, family, organisation, nation, economy and civilisation throughout the world. If removed, it will destroy the most powerful government, the most successful business, the most thriving economy, the most influential leadership, the greatest friendship, the strongest character and the deepest love. On the other hand, if developed and leveraged, this one thing has the potential to create unparalleled success and prosperity in every dimension of life. Yet, it is the least understood, most neglected, and most underestimated possibility of our time. This one thing is trust.

Trust impacts us 24/7 365 days of the year. It undergirds and affects the quality of every relationship, every communication, every work project, every business venture and every effort in which we are engaged. Contrary to what most people believe, trust is not some soft, illusive quality that you either have or you don't;

If you know someone who always seems to get their way, study them where possible and see how many techniques they are using.

The best persuaders do this effortlessly, often getting people round to their way of thinking before they realise it!

Trust impacts us 24/7 365 days of the year.

trust is a pragmatic, tangible, actionable asset that you can create.

When I refer to trust, I mean in the context of competence and character. Competence in the sense of the ability to do a task well and character defined by how a person does what they do. To make a distinction, a person may be a highly competent pilot, but if they have a habit of having a drink or two prior to a flight, crew members will soon be asking to be allocated to different flight routes. The pilot's character does not match his competence. Another example might be if an organisation has a no smoking policy in the office building, but the common knowledge is that the CEO smokes in his office. This is likely to be perceived as a rule for everyone else and another rule for the person in charge, and draw resentment. A third example is where a business leader suggests that employees are economical with the truth about features of a product when conversing with customers. This is likely to lead to backfiring if and when a customer expresses dissatisfaction with the functionality of the said product. No doubt, you get the point. These represent character flaws. It would be very difficult for any leader to gain real trust and influence following these types of scenarios.

When I refer to trust, I mean in the context of competence and character.

It would be very difficult for any leader to gain real trust and influence following these types of scenarios.

As we continue to move into an even more transparent, interdependent global reality, trust is more critical than it has ever been. Low trust causes friction, whether it is caused by unethical behaviour or by ethical but incompetent behaviour. Low trust creates hidden agendas, politics, interpersonal conflict, interdepartmental rivalries, win-lose thinking, defensive and protective communication. Low trust also slows everything down – every decision and every relationship.

On the other hand, trust produces speed, loyalty, repeat business, followers and strong partnerships.

Influence and persuasion in the absence of trust is almost an oxymoron.

As we continue to move into an even more transparent, interdependent global reality, trust is more critical than ever.

Influence and persuasion in the absence of trust is almost an oxymoron.

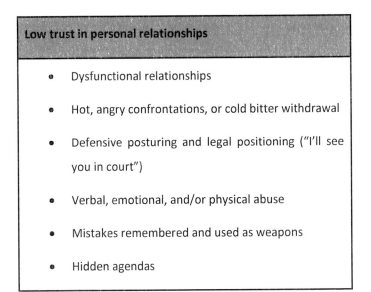

High trust in personal relationships

- Inspiring work done together

- Completely open, transparent relationships

- Mistakes seen as learning opportunities and quickly forgiven

- A focus on leveraging one another's strengths

- Polite, cordial healthy communications

Low trust in personal relationships

- Dysfunctional relationships

- Hot, angry confrontations, or cold bitter withdrawal

- Defensive posturing and legal positioning ("I'll see you in court")

- Verbal, emotional, and/or physical abuse

- Mistakes remembered and used as weapons

- Hidden agendas

Be liked...or at least be likeable

It is very rare that an unpleasant or downright nasty person finds success in influencing people. Of course in business, and life in general, there are points where we have to make decisions that upset people, but as long as we do them for the right reasons we won't be disliked. Being friendly to people, becoming genuinely interested in their lives and experiences, goes a long way towards forming the kind of bond that you need with someone should you wish to persuade them towards your way of thinking in the future. To put it in blunt terms, the stronger your bond with someone the more likely they are to be receptive to your ideas. There is of course no point in being nice if points are not well thought through. Ideas must be logical and make financial, economic or even common sense to influence or persuade.

Attitude

Your overall attitude during a conversation where you hope to exert influence over someone should be one of respect. You should respect their opinions, admit when you have made a mistake, and lead them gently round to your way of thinking rather than forcing your opinion on them from the start. No one likes a hard sell, so begin in a friendly manner, listen to the points they have to make in full and show that you have

It is very rare than an unpleasant or downright nasty person finds success in influencing people.

Being friendly to people, becoming genuinely interested in their lives and experiences, goes a long way.

There is of course no point in being nice if points are not well thought through.

Your overall attitude during a conversation where you hope to exert influence over someone should be one of respect.

considered their point of view, ideally by adopting a couple of their points into your perspective. If you can make them feel like the idea was theirs in the first place, you're onto a winner! If you both have fundamentally opposing views and you realise your opportunity is slipping away, don't force the issue – let it go and see if you can re-open the discussion at a later date. Chipping away with a trowel is more effective than hacking away with a pickaxe. One final point. It is best to develop a great attitude now. Trying to influence work colleagues following a promotion will be futile if all they can remember is the poor attitude you had before the big job came along. A great rule in life is to treat others as you would wish to be treated.

Language

Fundamentally, trying to persuade someone or influence their decision is like conducting a sale – you are trying to sell your point of view. This means that you must be the salesman – not always easy for a serial dodger! As we know, some people are natural sellers, but with practice you can utilise the same tools and apply them when required, the most crucial of which is language. A tool you may find useful is 'assumptive language'.

If you can make them feel like the idea was theirs in the first place, you're onto a winner!

Trying to influence work colleagues following a promotion will be futile if all they can remember is the poor attitude you had before the big job came along.

A great rule in life is to treat others as you would wish to be treated.

Assumptive language patterns assume the outcome of what you are asking. Imagine a scenario where you are trying to convince your boss to use your preferred supplier, Aggregates Ltd, and he asks why. You respond:

'I used Aggregates Ltd in the past because they're cheap and reliable. If you want I can call them to get a quote?'

You haven't really sold your supplier to your boss and you've left the decision to get a quote in his hands. You've also made it sound like it's a hassle for you to do so. As a result your boss is not going to be enthused by your idea. Now compare this with the following statement:

'If you use Aggregates Ltd I can guarantee they'll deliver what we need on time. They'll save us money compared to the current supplier and I know they're keen to work with us. Shall I call them now to get a quote?'

In the second instance you put across your supplier's qualities in a way that suggests there is no need to look elsewhere – your supplier fulfils all the key criteria and is better than the current one. You have used the assumption that your boss is going to agree

Assumptive language patterns assume the outcome of what you are asking.

You have used the assumption that your boss is going to agree.

to using your supplier (why wouldn't he, you've made them sound perfect!) to move to the next stage and 'seal the deal'. Here, you have phrased the suggestion to get a quote in such a way that it is harder for your boss to disagree with the suggestion, especially as you've offered to do the work – he has nothing to do, nothing to lose, and you are much more likely to get your desired outcome. You can see here how the same statement made in two very different ways will likely have two very different outcomes

Tone

As well as the language you use, the tone of voice is also important. Ending a sentence with an upward inflection suggests you are asking a question, whereas ending with a downward inflection indicates you're making a statement. Consider the request to call for a quote in the above example. Say the final line out loud with an upward inflection and then again with a downward inflection. The former allows the person answering the question to consider their answer and possibly reject it, whereas the latter comes across as a subtle command that it is easier to obey than to question. This is a very powerful way of encouraging someone to agree with your suggestions.

There are other tools you can employ to enhance your powers of influence and persuasion, from planting

As well as the language you use, the tone of voice is also important.

Using downward inflection is a very powerful way of encouraging someone to agree with your suggestions.

embedded commands to choosing the right posture to signify control, but these are more subtle methods that can be researched and tried once the above have been mastered.

Case Studies

These case studies have been included to help you with your preparation in becoming a Tackler not a Dodger. Please feel free to use them as part of your personal studies.

For copyright issues relating to using the case studies outside personal/home use, please contact the author at clive.lewis@tacklingdifficultconversations.com

Managing Difficult Conversations: Performance Management

Background

You work for a large FTSE250 organisation. Andy is a junior administrator in your team, and his performance in a number of areas is poor. He also happens to be the son of one of your directors who, when you previously broached the topic of Andy's underperformance, was dismissive of your concerns. You need to tackle this situation quickly; Andy's performance is having a negative effect on the team, but you are also aware you need to handle the delicate situation with his director father carefully.

The Issues

1. Andy is failing to meet deadlines, producing sloppy work and has an inadequate telephone manner. He is often up to 20 minutes late.

2. His poor performance is negatively impacting the rest of the team.

3. Andy's father, one of your directors, is dismissive of the issues.

4. You intend to put Andy on a Performance Improvement Plan (PIP), as per your company's procedures.

Your Task

You need to have two meetings – one with Andy and another with his director – to discuss the poor performance issues and the PIP you are hoping to implement. During the meetings, you will need to be mindful of the delicate family connections.

Managing Difficult Conversations: Patient/Clinician

Background

You oversee a number of doctors at an Acute Trust. On occasions, consultants from the hospital provide cover at a local hospice. You are one of these consultants. One afternoon you administer some medication to a patient at the hospice. The patient's notes indicated he was allergic to morphine, but somehow you manage to give morphine to the patient. You missed the notes. The effect was devastating. On a trip to the lavatory, the patient lost his balance and fell. The impact knocked his teeth through his lip and blackened his eyes. This is the lasting memory his wife and children have of their loved one, as he died a few days afterwards.

The family are aware that something was wrong with the medication given to the patient. Your colleague who also covers shifts at the hospice is also very angry with you and wants due process to take place. You are mortified. However, you have persuaded the chief executive of the hospice to allow you to have a conversation with the patient's family, to explain what happened to him. You also want to try and repair the relationship between you and your colleague.

The Issues

1. The family are considering legal action and want answers to some very serious questions.

2. You overlooked the patient's notes which stipulated that he was allergic to morphine.

3. Your colleague has postponed taking any further action until you have had a conversation with her.

Your Task

You must decide the best way to inform the patient's family of what has happened. You also need to have a discussion with your clinical colleague. Who should you talk to first and how should you approach both situations? Well planned and executed conversations may prevent further action – which could be legal.

Managing Difficult Conversations: Ben Gardiner – Personal hygiene

Background

Ben is the post room manager for a large clinical waste management company. The facilities department has just been put under your control and you are quickly aware that Ben's personal hygiene is a cause for concern. You have heard the odd mutter or two in your time at the company, but the truth is brought home after a meeting with him and his assistant, Gary: Ben's body odour, even first thing in the morning, is impossible to ignore.

You speak to HR about the issue and discover that Ben's previous assistant raised it with them last year, which led to Ben trying to tackle it. You speak to Gary privately, who says that it wasn't bad until three months ago when Ben divorced his wife. Gary says that working with Ben in such close quarters is now quite difficult, but on the one occasion he mentioned it Ben reacted very aggressively. Gary admits that he is looking for work elsewhere, but you think he could have a future at the company and don't want to lose him.

The Issues

1. Ben has a body odour problem which is causing his assistant, who you don't want to lose, to consider leaving the company.

2. It may have been spurred on by his divorce.

3. Ben is known to react negatively when the subject is broached.

Your Task

Engage with Ben about his body odour problem, choosing an appropriate setting and the best way to approach the subject

Managing Difficult Conversations: Underperforming supplier

Background

You work for an electronics manufacturer heading up the circuitry division, meaning you are responsible for ensuring the quality of the circuit boards and chips going into all the products. You have been working with the same microchip supplier for 15 years but you are getting pressure from the CEO to bring down costs. He has sourced cheaper suppliers and two of the last four batches of microchips from the existing supplier have been faulty and have had to be returned.

Your contact at the supplier is a personal friend and he has informed you that the company is losing contracts. You are aware that withdrawing your business could cause them significant damage, if not send them into administration. Your CEO has demanded that you call him and tell him that one more bad batch will result in the contract being terminated.

The Issues

1. The supplier your company has been using for 15 years are not meeting your requirements.

2. You have been asked to call them and inform them that if they supply one more poor batch and you will be cancelling the contract.

3. Your contact is a close personal friend.

4. Withdrawing your business could make the supplier go into administration.

Your Task

You need to speak to the supplier and inform them that they need to improve the quality of their products or they will lose the contract. Decide on an appropriate contact method, location and approach.

Conclusion

Hopefully this handbook has given you enough guidance and suggestions to begin tackling difficult conversations rather than dodging them. In whichever area of your life you are trying to make these changes, be they personal or professional, I can guarantee that once you have got into the groove of tackling difficult conversations all the little problems that previously caused you consternation and worry will be brought down to size and will now be given the short shrift they deserve. It is no overstatement to suggest that to serial dodgers this will represent a life changing shift, perhaps even transformation in attitude.

It seems too that companies have finally begun to realise the damage that dodger managers can do; a recent study found an encouraging 61.5% of employers increased manager training in the area of difficult conversations over a five year period[3]. This is a very positive statistic, but the fact still remains that there are thousands of managers out there who are unprepared to deal with situations when they arise, at huge cost to their respective organisations and the economy as a whole. As you have seen yourself, it really doesn't take much to become a tackler – just some willpower and the right guidance – and I'm sure you have already felt the benefits, or can at least see the plethora of benefits that tackling offers.

The amount of decisions that require our daily attention grows with age and experience, as does their variety and severity. Getting into the tackling groove as early as possible therefore is the best way forward before your aversion catches up with you. Your first few attempts at tackling difficult conversations may not work out exactly as you desire, but don't be put off.

Changing any embedded behaviour rarely meets with instant success, but the main thing is to concentrate on the positives and continue to try and kick your dodging habit instance by instance, to the point where you find that your reliance on this book and its methods takes second place to instinct and the effects of constant practice. Good luck!

References

[1] http://www.cedr.com/?location=/news/archive/20101109_356.htm

[2] http://www.xperthr.co.uk/article/105161/.aspx

[3] http://www.cipd.co.uk/hr-resources/survey-reports/conflict-management.aspx

Difficult Conversations:

10 Steps to Becoming a Tackler not a Dodger

In-house training courses

A high impact training course covering the key content areas of this handbook is available. It is the most popular non-mediation training course of all the suite of preventative training modules offered by Globis. Recent research shows that there has been a 61.5% increase in the number of companies offering training on difficult conversations. This handbook outlines 10 key steps to improve one's ability to be able to do this. The six hour training course provides hands-on practical skills whilst giving the opportunity to practice and observe real life case studies. Delegates will also benefit from being coached on how to deal with scenarios they are currently facing. This course offers highly valuable tips to meet the challenges faced by the world of work in the 21st century.

Hundreds of people have been delegates on this course, with 95% of attendees rating it 5/5. The content is highly interactive and the facilitators help delegates understand real truths in a no nonsense way. Each session is designed to run with between twelve and twenty-four delegates. It is suitable for anyone in the public, private or voluntary sectors. It is also applicable in non work settings.

To book an in-house training course or to find out more about other training programmes, call 0330 100 0809 or visit www.globis.co.uk.

Clive Lewis

Order form

Difficult Conversations
10 Steps to Becoming a Tackler not a Dodger

Book Quantity	Price
1-14 copies	£9.99 each
15-29 copies	£7.99 each
30-99 copies	£5.99 each
100-999 copies	£5.75 each
1,000-4,999 copies	£5.50 each
5,000-9,999 copies	£5.25 each
10,000 or more copies	£5.00 each
Audio Book CD Quantity	**Price**
1 (please call for multiple purchases)	£14.99

Name: ....   Job Title: ....

Organisation: ....

Address: ....

Postcode: ....   Tel No: ....

Email: ....

(Plus Postage and packing)
☐ Cheque enclosed (Please make payable to Globis Ltd)
☐ Please invoice
☐ Please debit my credit card

Name on card: ....   Card Number: ....

Start Date: ....   Expiry Date: ....   Security No: ....

Signed: ....

Post completed form to: Globis Ltd, Unit 1, Wheatstone Court, Quedgeley, Gloucester GL2 2AQ

Tel: 0330 100 0809
Fax: 01452 726001
Email: info@globis.co.uk

About the author

Clive Lewis is a UK based, leading Human Resources professional, specialising in employee and industrial relations. He is the founding director of Globis Mediation Group and Education HR Solutions. He is the author of 11 books including the widely acclaimed "Difficult Conversations – 10 Steps to Becoming a Tackler not a Dodger" which was featured in The Sunday Times. His work has taken him across four continents and he frequently works at Government level. He is Vice Chair of a leading Multi Academy Trust, a Non-Exec Director of an NHS Foundation Trust and a Trustee of the National Youth Jazz Orchestra.

He is heavily involved in charity work and devotes much of his time to helping young people from poor socio-economic backgrounds. His commitment to charity work led to him being appointed as Chair of a Government-appointed independent panel exploring the rising costs of youth underachievement.

He has recently launched the Bridge Builders mentoring scheme. The scheme connects schools with business to increase social mobility and employability amongst young men from poor backgrounds.

Notes

Notes